Life's Detours

Life's Detours

Wayne E. Oates

Library of Congress Catalog Card Number: 74-75221

The Scripture quotations in this publication, unless otherwise identified, are from the Revised Standard Version
Bible, copyrighted 1946, 1952 and © 1971 by the Division
of Christian Education, National Council of the Churches
of Christ in the United States of America.

The quotation from Martin Luther on page 5 is from *The
Table Talk of Martin Luther,* edited with an Introduction by
Thomas S. Kepler (New York & Cleveland: World Publishing
Co., 1952), p. 285.

We express our appreciation to the following who have granted
permission to reprint material from the books listed below:
Harper & Row, Publishers, Inc., for quotations from *The Living
of These Days: An Autobiography* by Harry Emerson Fosdick,
copyright © 1956 by Harper & Row, Publishers, Inc.; *The Hope
of the World* by Harry Emerson Fosdick (New York: Harper &
Row, 1933); *The Exploration of the Inner World* by Anton T.
Boisen (New York: Harper & Row, 1936); *Out of the Depths*
by Anton T. Boisen (New York: Harper & Row, 1960).

Princeton University Press for quotations from *A Short Life of
Kierkegaard* by Walter Lourie, copyright 1942 © 1970 by Princeton University Press.

Thomas Y. Crowell Company, Inc., for quotations from *Einstein:
The Life and Times* by Ronald W. Clark, copyright © 1971 by
Ronald W. Clark.

UR-306-10-0674
Printed in the United States of America

The Lord our God is a God of the humble and perplexed hearts, who are in need, tribulation and danger. If we were strong, we would be proud and haughty. God shows his power in our weakness; he will not quench the glimmering flax, neither will he break in pieces the bruised reed.

The Table Talk of Martin Luther

God keeps faith, and he will not allow you to be tested above your powers, but when the test comes he will at the same time provide a way out, by enabling you to sustain it.

1 Corinthians 10:13
The New English Bible

CONTENTS

CHAPTER I

Life's Detours

The direction we are going is largely affected by the way we interpret the things that happen to us. Our perception of things has a powerful effect upon what those things in fact turn out to be.

When our son Bill was about five years of age, I bought him a little balsam wood airplane. It was "powered" by a heavy rubber band. When twisted, the rubber band would unwind and turn the propeller. Thus the little plane flew well outside the house where there were no walls to hit. One day when the weather was bad, though, Bill was playing in the basement with his airplane. I heard him scream with anger. I went to the basement to see what had happened to him. He had attempted to fly his plane in the basement. It had crashed into pieces as it hit the basement wall. He was crying loudly, but all of a sudden he stopped crying and began to wipe his tears and even smile.

I asked him what had happened in his mind. He said: "I know what I will do; I will take that rubber band and make me a sling shot out of it!"

Bill is twenty-five now. He has served two tours of duty in Vietnam. He has seen the pieces, not only of real airplanes, but also of human lives. He himself has experienced pain and grief. Yet this story is a parable of his life. He has a way of grieving appropriately for a while. Then he sets about perceiving a new design, a new pattern, a new use of the pieces.

Life's detours do not just happen to individuals. Groups and communities come under the same weight of tragedy in the frustration of their chosen direction. They, too, are pushed to find a detour in direction. The people of Enterprise, Alabama, for example, were for decades a cotton-raising community. Cotton thrived well in this farming area. Then the boll weevil, an insect that destroys a cotton plant by infesting the cotton bolls, moved in with force and destroyed crop after crop. This disaster forced the farmers of Enterprise to go from a "one-crop economy"—cotton—to diversified farming. They discovered that peanuts, soybeans, cattle, and other livestock were even more advantageous and through diversification they could make a better living.

They were so grateful for this discovery that they erected a monument in Enterprise to the boll weevil! This lowly, accursed insect had at first been their destruction but then became their teacher and liberator from slavery to cotton! When you go to Enterprise, Alabama, look for the monument to the boll weevil.

These parables are one way of describing the point of this book: Life's fixed organizations, dreams, hopes, and fantasies have a way of slamming into walls and being smashed. A new way through, over, under, around, or out has to be found. The steadfast resolve under God to find that way results in a detour. Sometimes the detour takes us into directions we have never dreamed. The detour reveals to us that God is a God of fresh alternatives. God does not foreordain that evil and disastrous things happen to us. Rather, he works *after the fact* of tragedy through our powers of perception to reveal to us new avenues of growth, hope, opportunity, and realization. We would never have found these new ways if our eyes had not been jarred open by untoward and dark events.

Biblical Cases of Life's Detours

We need to look for biblical perspectives for handling life's detours. When we do so, we can turn to two persons, Joseph and Moses.

Joseph in Egypt

At the age of seventeen, Joseph was a dreamer. He saw no limits to his dreams and visualized himself as ruling over his brothers and parents. He dreamed that they would bow down to him. His dreams got him into trouble with his brothers who first proposed to kill him. But they threw him into a pit and then retrieved him and sold him into slavery. Slavery itself seemed a fresh and hopeful alternative after being thrown into a waterless pit to die.

The dreams that had gotten Joseph into trouble became a fresh detour for him. By interpreting the dreams of men all the way to the Pharaoh himself, Joseph, a wounded healer of people in trouble through the interpretation of their dreams, used the suffering he had endured to help others. He became a servant of others rather than a lord over them.

Finally, the forward-looking providence of God led Joseph's brothers back to him. He ministered to them rather than placing himself above them. When he revealed himself to them, he gave his own interpretation of his life in relation to God:

"I am your brother, Joseph, whom you sold into Egypt. And now do not be distressed, or angry with yourselves, because you sold me here; for God sent me before you to preserve life" (Genesis 45:4-5).

Moses in Egypt

Moses was moved deeply by the mistreatment of his people. He sought to set them free through violence and killed a man in the process. He had to flee for his own life. He was a murderer in his own right. He "lay low" for years as a herder of sheep and as one who meditated in the long watches of the day and night in the wilderness.

Yet God had not forgotten him. He was preparing a new way of intervention for the people of Israel in bondage in Egypt. His intention was to rely upon this same Moses. His way of doing so was to send Moses into the wilderness for a long detour. The tutelage of his silence in the wilderness, the wisdom of Jethro, his father-in-law, the instruction of nature, the experience of marriage and parenthood, and the mellowing of his perception of himself as a leader all took place during one of life's detours. The intervening years between the time Moses "killed the Egyptian and hid him in the sand" (Exodus 2:12) and the time the Lord spoke to him at the burning bush made Moses a wise as well as righteous man. This long detour would seem to us to be not a detour but the end of life. We would at a certain point in Moses' career brand him as a criminal and write him off for any future contribution to life. We would keep a careful record of his past and see this as the end of the road rather than a detour in life for him.

Yet God thinks differently. Our God is a God of ingenuity and persistence with us as human beings. He uses such occasions as Moses' violent anger as catalysts of new directions in living. These events are not the end of life's way. They are points of "wheeling about" one hundred eighty degrees, ninety degrees, forty-five degrees, or even ten degrees to be corrected on course later. A ten-degree course change now can make an amazing change in the point of arrival ten or twenty years from now.

Erik Erikson has said that the maturation process of late adolescents calls for a "psychological moratorium" in which they take some deliberate detours from the heavily programmed "freeways" of high school, college, etc., before they come to closure on permanent life commitments of vocation, marriage, and parenthood. If parents and teachers do not collaborate with this detouring and wandering process, then life has a way of catalyzing circumstances that will force detours. Apparently, the very successful Moses had been carefully programmed in the rituals and education of Egyptian royalty. His true being and identity began emerging. No one around him heard the cries of his destiny. Chaotic behavior changed the course of his prepackaged and preplanned life. The creative God moved into the chaos and brought a new direction to his life. For all who observed, and probably for Moses himself, this new direction *looked* like a detour. From God's point of view, though, the wrath of man was being made to praise God the Creator. God does not give up on men and women so easily or so quickly as we give up on ourselves and each other.

Some Laws of Life's Detours

The detours of life are not willy-nilly, lawless, and without basic principle beneath their operation. Therefore, we need to do two things here. First, we need to identify some of the laws of action upon which effective and prayerful discovery of life's detours is based. Second, in the rest of the book, we need to demonstrate the reality of life's detours in actual life stories of people who had wit and consecration, "who through faith conquered kingdoms, enforced justice, received promises, stopped the mouths of lions, quenched raging fire, escaped the edge of the sword, won strength out of weakness, became mighty in war, put foreign armies to flight" (Hebrews 11:33-34). At this point in time, the basic laws of life's detours need attention. What are some of them? I can name a few, and you will probably name others from your own detours in life.

The Law of Compensation

Alfred Adler, the psychologist who parted company with Sigmund Freud, made a discovery which he called "psychical compensation." He noted, for example, that when one part of the body is removed, such as a kidney, a lung, an eye, the other companion of that part tends to strengthen and take over the functions of the lost part. Or, if one whole sense, such as sight, is lost, then the senses of touch and hearing are sharpened and used all the more.

The life of Helen Keller is an example of the way in which the sense of sight and hearing were rechanneled into touch. Only recently have Gestalt psychologists begun to develop experiments in sensory awareness that take persons with *all* of their sense organs intact and teach them to use the senses of touch, smell, and vision more abundantly rather than to be sensorily deprived by allowing potentials to go unused. We are a hearing-oriented people and do not enrich life through the use of all of our senses. Compensation is a detour of life that deals with the reality of loss— the loss of a part of the body; the loss of a loved one by separation, divorce, abandonment, or death; the loss of a job, a cause, or an ideal, etc.

Another way of stating the law of compensation is through what Horace Bushnell called the "moral use of dark things." He says that life's negatives, weaknesses, and limitations can be *used* creatively and turned into positives, strengths, and potentials. The Book of Hebrews calls it "winning strength out of weakness." Ralph Waldo. Emerson, in his essay *Compensation,* states it this way:

Our strength grows out of weakness. Not until we are pricked and stung and sorely shot at, awakens the indignation which arms itself with secret forces. A great man is always willing to be little. Whilst he sits on the cushion of advantage, he goes to sleep. When he is pushed, tormented, defeated, he has a chance to learn something; he has been put on his wits, on his manhood; he has gained facts; learns his ignorance; is cured of the insanity of conceit; has got moderation and skill. The wise man always throws himself on the side of his assailants. It is more to his interest than to theirs to find his weak point. . . . In general, every evil to which we do not succumb, is a benefactor."

The Law of Realism

The first impulse one has in the face of a detour in life is to develop a Pollyanna attitude of "positive thinking" that denies the reality of what has really happened to us. In fact, all that I have said here could easily be interpreted as a "positive mental attitude" effort to make a sufferer feel better. To a certain extent, such denial as a coping mechanism is necessary to get us through the initial shock of a loss, a grief, a disappointment, a frustration, a calamity. In this sense, "positive thinking" is a necessary part of the management of a detour in life.

Beyond the initial stages of shock and numbness, though, denial becomes a form of fantasy and unreality. When a friend or loved one completely rejects us, excoriates us, and tells us we are one hundred percent evil and no good, *at first* it is a helpful thing to make excuses for him or her, to say that he or she is just upset, does not really mean it, etc. But to adopt this form of excuse-making and denial as a permanent way of life ignores the basic law of reality. The person really *does* reject us. Nothing can be done about it. Only a clean break with our dreams and a frank acceptance of reality provides a realistic basis for discovery of a new way. Only then can our perception see a new design in the pieces, a new way through the tragedy, a new direction of creativity in the chaos.

We have to admit that the pieces are *there* before anything can be made of them. We have to admit that we are lost before we set ourselves seriously about finding a fresh alternative route for our lives. The very idea of a detour presupposes the acceptance of the reality of a hopeless, nonviable route that has been forfeited once and for all. This realism is hard to come by for travelers along life's way. A sign at an intersection of a highway said: "Detour. Bridge out 3 miles ahead." A head-strong motorist said: "Oh, well! I am in a hurry. I'll bet I can make it." So he ignored the facts the sign gave him and drove on anyway. He came to the impassable bridge. Another sign said: "The Bridge *IS* Out, Isn't It!" People can give us facts. They can advise us about new routes for a detour. They can comfort us in our frustration and the pain of our disappointment. They can even exhort us that we *ought* not to continue in an old, self-defeating way. They can lose patience with our headstrongness. We can continue to act as if that which is *so* is not really so.

Life itself, though, only gives us facts. Life does not advise, comfort, exhort, or lose patience. Neither does it take any wrongheadedness on our part in response to the facts it gives. God through the Holy Spirit is everready to respond with answers to our asking for a detour in life. He is always eager to open new doors when we knock. He is always providing fresh alternatives for those who seek them. So ask, seek, and find.

A person who has lost someone by divorce has the most obvious difficulty with this dimension of reality in the dark experience of a broken marriage. To live in fantasy is the first option. It is not a viable option, though, but only a temporary assuagement of the hurt that, like morphine in surgery, has to be withdrawn. Otherwise, our religion will become as Marx said it was, "the opium of the people." It was our Lord Jesus Christ who could say that he had indeed been forsaken and also refused the luxury of a perception of life without a cross when he all the while was dying to an old life to be resurrected to a new one.

The Law of Perspective

The capacity to see the ridiculous, the audacious, the funny, and the humorous points to another law of life for the discovery of creative life detours. Accurate perspective amounts to standing off far enough from a set of events to see them in perspective, as a whole, with every part set in right relationship to every other part. Sometimes the law of perspective results in humor, at others in a sense of beauty. A young machine gunner in Vietnam in 1968 spoke of being in a firefight at night. The horror of the battle around him was intense. However, the multicolored array of tracer bullets suddenly took on a beauty in the dark that gave him a perspective of life that enabled him to avoid being overwhelmed by the horror of battle. Futhermore, the sense of awe and mystery in caring love provides a new alternative route for being a person. For example, a young patient who is facing the diagnosis of cancer becomes concerned about the well-being of her parents and brothers and sisters and devotes her attention to them.

Caring for them helps her to maintain her own perspective of what is happening to her.

An older word for perspective is *wisdom*. The Book of Proverbs advises: "Say to wisdom, 'you are my sister,' and call insight your intimate friend" (Proverbs 7:4). In another place, the Book says:

> My son, keep sound wisdom and discretion;
>   let them not escape from your sight,
> and they will be life for your soul
>   and adornment for your neck.
> Then you will walk on your way securely
>   and your foot will not stumble.
> If you sit down, you will not be afraid;
>   when you lie down, your sleep will be sweet.
> Do not be afraid of sudden panic,
>   or of the ruin of the wicked, when it comes;
> for the Lord will be your confidence
>   and will keep your foot from being caught.
>   Proverbs 3:21-26

The law of perspective is another way of describing patience, a word that comes from the Greek word for suffering or pain. "Putting up with things" calls for a certain kind of perspective. Enduring suffering and pain produces a certain kind of wisdom in its own right. Pain makes you think. Thought makes you wise. Wisdom makes pain bearable.

The Law of Resurrection

Even before the Christian era of commitment to the risen Lord Jesus Christ, the Egyptians had the story of the Phoenix. Life arises out of the ashes of destruction. In the Old Testament, the Book of Isaiah describes the way in which the powers of redemption from the eternal God work

in the ruins of life to bring order out of chaos, peace out
of war, gladness out of mourning:

> The Spirit of the Lord God is upon me,
>   because the Lord has anointed me
> to bring good tidings to the afflicted;
>   he has sent me to bind up the brokenhearted;
> to proclaim liberty to the captives,
>   and the opening of the prison to those who are bound;
> to proclaim the year of the Lord's favor
>   and the day of vengeance of our God;
>   to comfort all who mourn;
> to grant to those who mourn in Zion—
>   to give them a garland instead of ashes,
> the oil of gladness instead of mourning,
>   the mantle of praise instead of a faint spirit;
> that they may be called oaks of righteousness,
>   the planting of the Lord, that he may be glorified.
> They shall build up the ancient ruins,
>   they shall raise up the former devastations;
> they shall repair the ruined cities,
>   the devastations of many generations.
>
>   Isaiah 61:1-4

The redemptive power of our Lord Jesus Christ incar-
nates in human form the way in which he committed his
life to a path and a way that was built upon the conviction
that though he was crucified and buried he would rise again.
The apostle Paul saw this not just as an event that called
for biological death, an event that would be overcome in
the hereafter. Paul saw this as a law of life. We are being
killed all the day long. Every day we are being crucified
with Christ, nevertheless we are raised to walk in the newness of life. The Resurrection is a law of daily life. Lost
people finding their way is a neat transaction for saying the
right words at the right time in a church service. The

pilgrimage of life does not take place once and for all at a pinpoint in time. Shattering and wasting things happen to us all along the way. An old life has to die repeatedly and a new one is born. The circumscribing idolatries of life do fall apart. The way of life we build around them lapses, falls into the ground, and dies. The reason for this is revealed in Jesus' words, ". . . unless a grain of wheat falls into the earth and dies, it remains alone" (John 12:24). If, to the contrary, it is planted, it may bring forth a hundredfold.

The detours of life often are begun by a dead end. We literally back out and start all over again. The death of a direction is the birth of a new one. The *law of resurrection* is the law of life, and it is written into the scarred tissue of humanity. Old things must pass away *in order that* all things may be made new. Much of our kicking, screaming, complaining, depression, and projection of blame onto others is little more than our steadfast refusal to "get with life" and our desire to hang on to a patently dead past. We die a little or a lot when our way of life no longer moves us into a fuller relationship to God, to ourselves, and to others. The self that dies through such faith will be raised to a new life through the revealing power of God.

The Law of Fellowship

God meets us as individuals when a chosen way of life has had its day and begins to cease to be. He does so through spontaneous insight from the recesses of our own beings. He does so through the behavior, words, and sustaining grace of other people. They are our "life support system" and often serve as "mission control" when we are thrown off course on an ever-so-carefully-planned adventure. The Skylab experiment ran into trouble from the moment of lift-off. The astronauts began immediately to advise alternative procedures and ultimately improvised ways of accomplishing tasks. This they could not have done without a ground control and support system.

The fellowship of Christians is the life support community of the individual as he or she recharts his or her course. The church at its best is in the world to minister and not to be ministered unto. We restore each other gently when we overtake each other in a fault. We bear one another's burdens and so fulfill the law of Christ. We each bear our own burdens. When burdens are grievous to be borne, we together cast them upon the Lord, for we know he cares for us. When any one of us begins to lose his or her way, the rest of us are available as guides in the wilderness of the lost. We work at devising new detours. The ultimate goal is the New Jerusalem. The variety of roads there is always being multiplied by the Trailblazer of our faith, Jesus Christ our Lord.

The situations of life described in the following pages point to ways in which these laws of life's detours are actually worked out in the lives of both well-known and not so well-known people. In all instances, they are real people. Positive examples outweigh negative evidence.

CHAPTER II

Winning Strength
Out of Weakness

Rollo May tells us that one of the serious maladies of today is the pervasive sense of powerlessness which characterizes many people. The Vietnam War created massive confusion. Confusion in the leadership of our country and the impersonal character of the decision making processes in schools, governments, churches, etc., dishearten us. People tend to throw up their hands in helplessness. They feel that there is nothing they can do about anything.

Furthermore, the mass media pound one's eyes and ears with stimuli. Increased population reduces the amount of opportunity that people have for solitude. Increased automobile traffic multiplies the road hazards with noise and fumes. People become over-stimulated, keyed up, and excited by the multiplicity of directions in which they could possibly go. They become so over-stimulated that they are powerless to choose between the multiple demands facing them. In the presence of these kinds of pressures, a sense of weakness overwhelms people.

The prophet Isaiah put it this way:

> Even youths shall faint and be weary,
> and young men shall fall exhausted.
> Isaiah 40:30

It is comforting to know that the generation of Isaiah and our generation are not the only ones who have been faced by the situation which has just been described. At the turn of this century, Harry Emerson Fosdick, longtime pastor of the Riverside Church in New York, was a young man studying philosophy and theology at Columbia University. He was working intensively in mission work in the Bowery section of New York. He worked in the humid heat of New York City without respite. He took no exercise. He had a devastating schedule as he helped to run the mission at Mariner's Temple in the Bowery. He says that he saw face to face the "down and out riffraff" of the city, from "constitutional ne'er-do-wells to Yale Phi Beta Kappa persons done in by drink." He says that he began his ministry in the raw filth, poverty, and degradation of the Bowery, "worse than is easily imaginable now." He learned much about the social situation, but his heavy load proved too much for him. He tells his own story in the following words from his autobiography, *The Living of These Days:*

One night in late November I could not sleep. It was the beginning of the most hideous experience of my life.

I have no intention of shadowing those recollections with a full account of that dreadful time. I suppose I had a nervous breakdown coming to me. High-strung and sensitive, I was built for one, and the experience was not unfamiliar to my family. It was not trouble that slew me but happiness—the excitement of the most exhilarating opportunity I had ever had. After a few days and nights of sleepless, agonizing tension, I fled to Worcester, hoping that a brief respite in my fiancée's company would set me to rights. Instead, I went from bad to worse. Then I fled to Buffalo, a humiliated nervous wreck, returning to be an emotional and financial burden on a home from which so recently I had gone forth with flags flying.

Many times in later years I have faced people who started in to tell me the inner hell of their neurotic agony—the waves of melancholia, the obsessive anxieties, the desire for suicide and all the rest—and I have stopped them, saying: "Don't you tell me, let me tell you how you feel." One typical man, with wide eyes, exclaimed when I was through: "My God! How did you know that?" [1]

Dr. Fosdick tells of his gradual release from his "pit of utter despair":

After months of perdition, my physician insisted that I be sent to some rest cure, and so I found myself in a sanitarium in Elmira, New York. I shrink yet at the thought of what that meant to my family. Raymond and Edith [his siblings] were in college, and I, who should have been on my own, was eating deeper and deeper into the family's capacity to borrow money at the bank. After a few weeks at the sanitarium, however, the head physician began canceling all bills in return for my tutoring of his son in Latin, and that eased my mind. Slowly but surely recovery progressed, and after four months I was set free and hurried to Worcester to see my long-suffering and worried fiancée. I was a poor risk to be engaged to at that stage of the game. With casual acquaintances I passed as normal, but anyone under the same roof with me could see that I was nervously ragged still. Then my father-in-law to be—one of the best men I ever knew—sent me to Europe.

It was a six weeks' trip—long days each way on cattle steamers and three weeks in England—and it marked the turning of the tide. Stratford-on-Avon is chiefly notable to me not as Shakespeare's birthplace but because for two nights running I got there long nights of natural sleep. I began to see hope ahead. . . .

.   .   .   .

This whole horrid experience was one of the most important factors in my preparation for the ministry. For the first time in my life, I faced, at my wit's end, a situation too much for me to handle. I went down into the depths where self-confidence becomes ludicrous. There the technique I had habitually relied upon—marshaling my wit and my volition and going strenuously after

[1] Harry Emerson Fosdick, *The Living of These Days: An Autobiography*. Copyright © 1956 by Harper & Row, Publishers, Inc., pp. 72-73. Used by permission of Harper & Row.

what I wanted—petered completely out. The harder I struggled, the worse I was. It was what I did the struggling with that was sick. I, who had thought myself strong, found myself beaten, unable to cope not only with outward circumstances but even with myself." [2]

This was a severe soul-shaking detour in life for the aggressive, self-confident, accustomed-to-success Fosdick. All of his "starch" was taken out of him by the experience. Yet, it was a time of turning and learning. It was a time of re-charting his direction in life. It was a time of discovering new resources for living. In his further reflections upon this experience, Fosdick identifies ways in which the experience itself was a preparation for being a Christian minister. This came about in several different ways. He learned several different things in this struggle of the soul.

Learning to Pray

Fosdick had grown up in a tightly orthodox tradition. He tells of being a boy seven years of age, crying himself to sleep at night in terror lest, dying, he should go to hell. Nevertheless, in his home he had a loving and comforting mother, and in its own way a little Baptist church gave him a sense of the world field that was "big enough to keep a map of the world before the eyes of its people" and to inspire him as a little boy to want to be a missionary.

Yet both his early orthodoxy and his later liberalism were based upon a clear rationalism. The experience which he in his own words described of his nervous breakdown shattered this overconfident rationalism. It turned him to prayer. He says:

---

[2] *Ibid.*, pp. 73-75.

I learned to pray, not because I had adequately argued out prayer's rationality, but because I desperately needed help from a Power greater than my own. I learned that God, much more than a theological proposition, is an immediately available Resource; that just as around our bodies is a physical universe from which we draw all our physical energy, so around our spirits is a spiritual Presence in living communion with whom we can find sustaining strength. Without that experience I do not think I would have written one of my early books, *The Meaning of Prayer*.[3]

This book of which Fosdick speaks went through thirty-eight printings and sold more than a half-million copies. Prayer is described in his book as a natural communion with God who cares for the individual. It calls for persistence in the face of difficulties. Fosdick gives us the following lesson that he learned about prayer:

Make up your mind in advance to keep your course steady, *when you feel like it and when you don't.* This difficulty of moods has been met by all God's people. . . .
    "A man who surrenders to these variable moods is doomed to inefficiency. He is like a ship that drifts as the tides run and the winds blow, and does not hold its course through them and in spite of them." [4]

Dr. Fosdick continues, "Many a life, like an old-fashioned well, has latent resources of living water underneath, but the pump needs priming. Into a man's prayerless mood let a little living water from someone else's prayer be poured, and water from the nether wells of the man's own soul may flow again." [5]

Therefore, one can learn from what Fosdick learned during his great life's detour: to pray.

---

[3] *Ibid.,* p. 75.
[4] Harry Emerson Fosdick, *The Meaning of Prayer* (New York: Association Press, 1940), pp. 81-82.
[5] *Ibid.,* pp. 82-83.

Learning About Human Nature

Fosdick says that during his life's detour which has been described above he "learned as well much about human nature that academic courses in psychology leave out." Human nature became to him living documents for study and encounter. In one of his sermons at Riverside he says:

> Do not suppose that because on Sunday you see a minister in a black gown perched in the carved pulpit of a Gothic church, that he does not know. A working minister can sometimes see more of the seamy side of life in a week than a roué sees in a month; for the roué may see only his own rottenness, but the minister in intimate disclosure will see the deep and varied iniquity of man.[6]

Fosdick's unusual approach to preaching can be systematized into a psychological understanding of the person before God. He measured the effectiveness of his preaching by the number of individuals who sought counseling afterward. He, more than any other American preacher, laid down the runways for the coming of pastoral care and counseling as a disciplined application of the sciences of human nature to the work of the minister in the care and/or cure of the growing and/or sick soul. The knowledge he gained for this work, however, came into being, according to him, as a direct result of his long, torturous detour in a nervous breakdown. The breakdown was a detour, not a permanent way of life. He learned every step of the way of his detour and, as expressed in the words of his hymn "God of Grace and God of Glory," found new hope "for the living of these days."

---

[6] Harry Emerson Fosdick, *The Hope of the World* (New York: Harper & Row, 1933), p. 46. Used by permission.

A Shift of Center

Fosdick attributes a real shift of center in his vocational purpose in life to the harrowing experience of his emotional collapse. Prior to this experience he said, "Fewer winnings and more defeats would have been salutary. I may have been heading for the ministry, but I was not distinguished for meekness." [7] The influence of a divinity school professor helped him decide to be a minister. Dr. Fosdick writes about his decision: "I was sure at last that I would be a minister, not a preacher but a teacher, perhaps of comparative religion." [8]

However, after the severe suffering which he encountered as he took the intellectualisms of his philosophical and theological training into the heavy demands of the Mariner's mission, he says:

I began to want to preach.

This shift of center from a teaching to a preaching ministry began during my breakdown. That was an experience fit to shake a man out of any intellectual conceit he may have had and make him face up to human problems of another kind. One effect of it on me was to make me want to get at folks—ordinary, everyday folks—and try to help them. It was a wide shift of emphasis. . . . Although I had an acquisitive mind and plenty of mental curiosity, creative scholarship would not have been my forte. My vocation was to be an interpreter in modern, popular, understandable terms, of the best that I could find in the Christian tradition. Humbled and chastened by a harrowing experience, and enlightened by study at a great seminary, I turned with increasing eagerness toward that calling.[9]

---

[7] Fosdick, *The Living of These Days*, p. 60.

[8] *Ibid.*, p. 66.

[9] *Ibid.*, p. 78.

Nevertheless, Fosdick's experience of inward suffering in his breakdown, following heavy grief over the death of his mother, did not dull the edge of his scholastic commitment. He later returned to a professorship at Union Theological Seminary. He did this concurrently with his task as a disciplined preacher in the pulpit of Riverside Church. He says: "The thing I am proudest about in my scholastic record is that despite the handicap of my nervous collapse, the seminary gave me a *summa cum laude*." [10] Obviously, the deep toning of his spiritual life, the enriching tower of a life of prayer and utter dependence upon the resources of the living God, and the chastened awareness of his own limitations and weaknesses had in nowise dulled Fosdick's devotion to his studies.

It would not be wise to devote too much of this book to the life of ministers. This would cause the reader to assume that these are the kinds of things that happen only to people who enter the Christian ministry and stay in it. To the contrary, many other persons in other walks of life will be studied as to the power of great reversals in life to change the sense of direction, shape their personal commitment, and enrich the quality of service that they give to people. Nevertheless, it is worthy of noting at the outset that one of this century's most revered and influential preachers crashed into the abutments of his own limitations, suffered great weakness and calamity, and yet arose to find a new direction in prayer, in the knowledge of human nature, and in the proclamation of the Word of God. That man was Harry Emerson Fosdick. In the conclusion of his autobiography, he says:

---

[10] *Ibid.*, p. 80.

My grandson, Steve, wrote for his school class a poem about the ocean, whose closing lines run:

> Ah, thou Neptune! Thou dost govern
> All the stormy sea around;
> But even in thy strength and fury
> Sleepy harbors can be found.[11]

Fosdick continues by saying:

That is a sage observation from an eleven-year-old. But, despite the tranquil harbors, this generation has no place for "intrepid complacency."

Nevertheless, at threescore-years-and-eighteen I find this generation the most stimulating, exciting, provocative—yes, promising —era I have ever seen or read about. I am not yet ready to die. I want to see what is going to happen next. Like the French editor, carried in a tumbrel through the streets of Paris to the guillotine, I would say: "It is too bad to cut off my head; I want to see how all this is coming out." Prophetic, germinative ideas are here; there are open doors of possibility for good as well as evil, which did not exist when I was born; and though I am an old man, I share at least a little the hopeful spirit of the young, facing life, as Lowell sang, with "the rays of morn on their white shields of Expectation!" [12]

Travelers' Cues for Detours

You and I as travelers on a spiritual pilgrimage of our own can gather several cues from Fosdick's experiences that will stay with us as we meet experiences similar to his.

First, enthusiasm and overconfidence seemed to have run away with Fosdick. He became so excited by the possibilities of life that he ignored the limitations of time and energy that life sets for everyone. We are not gods. We are human.

---

[11] *Ibid.*, pp. 318-319.
[12] *Ibid.*, p. 319.

We have the necessities of sleep, rest, diversion, and the acceptance of the necessities to face as a part of our discipline as travelers of the pilgrimage God has set before us. Fosdick seemed to have been running the race of life as if it were a hundred-yard dash. In reality it was a cross-country run. His collapse taught him this. We can learn this from him. It *is* a long pull.

Second, Fosdick did not get impatient with himself or give up just because he had been stymied. Rather, he chose to learn from what was happening to him in order that he might understand himself and human nature generally in a much more thorough and human, down-to-earth way. Therefore, when we become anxious, depressed, and shattered, we can learn from this not to become more anxious and depressed and shattered because we are this way. Our perfectionism may say that this can happen to everyone else but us. We lose patience with ourselves for being human. Fosdick had the courage of his own imperfections and recognized the bounds of his habitations. Hence he could write from his own experience about "being a real person."

Finally, Fosdick seemed to have the capacity to stand off and look at himself rather objectively even though he was suffering. God took this objectivity and enabled him to regain his perspective through it. This is a far, far better thing than simply adopting a "nervous" outlook as a way of life. If you and I are tempted to adopt our collapsed situation as a way of life, we would do well to look around the edges of it and see if we are not getting something out of it in the way of a side gain that we don't want to give up. We may be getting the control of our home situation when without our symptoms we will have to join up and be just another one of the family. We may be avoiding responsibility that would make us happier if we "got with it" and discharged the obligations that, unpleasant as they are, nevertheless are ours. Or, we may know very well what we need to be doing to get out of the plight we are in but lack the courage to implement our convictions. We can learn from Fosdick that getting out of such a predicament can very well teach us many things about ourselves that we desperately need to know in order to be real persons.

CHAPTER III

Setting at Liberty the Captives

Harry Emerson Fosdick was a silver-tongued orator, a preacher par excellence. He suffered the severe life's detour of a nervous breakdown. Yet this detour led him to the great territory of prayer, the psychological understanding of religious experience, and the care and counseling of troubled persons.

The person about whom I am going to tell you now is a layman. He is a man who only occasionally appears before public audiences. I cannot tell you his real name because he is concerned about an untoward effect that putting his name in print might have upon his family. Therefore, I will give him a biblical name, Barnabas. I chose this name because this man is a person who encourages and puts heart into others.

Barnabas comes from a highly respected family. He cared tenderly for his parents until their death. He now lives in a beautiful home he and his wife built high on a hill that is a part of the old estate of his parents. His wife, who stood by him through thick and thin for twenty-six years, is dead. He lives alone in the house now—alone with memories of a pilgrimage that was detoured drastically by a term spent in prison when he was about thirty years of age. These memories flash back to the occasion of his imprisonment.

Barnabas was and is in the stocks and bonds business. I do not know the heartbreaking details of the events that led up to his imprisonment. I do know that he was accused of some sort of mismanagement of funds, convicted of a criminal charge, and sentenced to the state prison for a term of five years. He served two and a half years. I know enough about the specific charges to know that as of today the laws are such that he would never have been charged, much less convicted. I also know that he had a plea of guilty entered against his will by his lawyer. This resulted in a precipitous and no doubt unjust conviction. Nevertheless, he went to prison.

These heartbreaking events are only the prelude to what really happened, though. The prison cell in which he lived was only a little bit larger than the cot upon which Barnabas slept. He says that his relationship to God became the most important process of happenings going on while he was in prison. He says that the Holy Spirit became as real to him as another human being without any of the silly foolishness he hears people attributing to the Holy Spirit today. He felt his loneliness and his fear overcome by the presence of the Holy Spirit. He felt the exhausted springs of hope being replenished by the assurance and comfort of the Holy Spirit. Prayer ceased to be a formality and became the very breath of his life.

Barnabas says that before his imprisonment, he had been a faithful churchgoer. He had always been relatively active in his church. He had appreciated his Bible and sought to live a good life. Withal, however, religion as a part of being customary with other people was never like what was happening to him in prison. He had time to meditate in prison and began to develop a contemplative life.

The seeds of contemplation had been sown in Barnabas' early, formal religious training. Yet the struggle of the working world and the busyness of the business world pre-

vented these seeds from germinating. They began to sprout
and put forth tender shoots in the days of Barnabas' imprisonment. The solace of the presence of the Holy Spirit
nourished his soul. The companionship of the Holy Spirit
let him know the powerful secret of turning destructive
loneliness into creative solitude. The instruction of the Holy
Spirit became his guide and teacher as he collected observa-
tions and arranged them into decisions.

Barnabas' experience of the Holy Spirit did not stop as
a private soliloquy with God. He did not remain in an
unintelligible "private ownership" of a secret with God. Of
course, the prison cell assigned to Barnabas and the cot on
which he lay were his "closet" in which he had—much
against his own will—been closeted. But there were *other*
cells and *other* men in that prison. Barnabas began to reach
out toward them.

As Barnabas quietly observed the life of the prison, he
saw that the inmates were like sheep without a shepherd,
harried and helpless. They had only a politically appointed
"preacher" and no one with whom they could converse.
The chaplains were "ears" for the politicians more than they
were "ears" for the still sad music of humanity in the
poignant lives of the inmates and their families. One such
chaplain at the prison is reported reliably as having said:
"I can't get a thing done for these men stopping me and
wanting to tell me their troubles!"

Barnabas then had another experience with God. One
day he walked in the prison yard and saw hundreds of men
standing around—indolent, defeated, bored, and hostile. It
came to him as a waste, and worse, a crime in its own right.
It was a crime against the dignity of man and the image of
God within the men to let lives mark time in bitterness and
uselessness this way. The great force of feelings of injustice

within Barnabas began to find a new direction. Barnabas could not explain why, but he resolved then and there—more than forty years ago—"to try to do something about it." What was originally a stalling, frustrating detour that literally ground Barnabas' life to a halt was now becoming the opening of a new way and a new depth to Barnabas. A later interviewer describes Barnabas' experience this way after he conferred with him. At many points he quotes Barnabas.

In Earlier Days Worked Alone

It happens every week; sometimes two or three times. It's been happening that way for forty years.

In all that time, Barnabas has been working to help the men, women, and youngsters in his state's institutions. At first he worked alone, making speeches, buttonholing citizens, talking with officials—always in the interest of prison reform.

Later he worked through the various institutions and committees of councils of churches.

It has been a long, plodding, sometimes discouraging endeavor, seeking to move away from the condition as Barnabas first saw it—prisons totally dominated by politics, inmates hung by their arms for hours at a time, a system devoted merely to keeping men locked up for a prescribed time with no thought of rehabilitation.

He has had to walk the tenuous tightwire between political interests, endure the apathy of people who would just as soon forget the men behind bars, suffer the disappointment of seeing men fail and fail again.

There has been no money and no prestige in what he was doing. He could have followed a hundred other more rewarding lines. But his interest never flagged; his effort was steadfast.

Doing Something for Somebody

Why? Why would a man with an investment-counseling business that moves him into the circles of the hardworking and law-abiding devote so much time to such opposites?

Barnabas will laugh a bit if you ask him, poke ashes from a pipe that never seems to get lit, and say:

"Well, it's my golf and my bridge, my recreation. It's the accomplishment of doing something for somebody else."

But merely filling time or satisfying pride isn't enough of an answer. A bit closer to the truth is the fact that he saw a need.

Why he vowed to do something about it grew out of what he is and where he came from. He grew up in a Christian home and was taught to live the Christian life. Common terms, those, with different meanings for different people.

Could Not Ignore Conditions

To Barnabas it meant that he could not look upon the needful condition of his fellowman and turn his back. He had to do something, and that purposefulness is part of what makes an apostle. It is something like the ambition that drives some men toward money or success or pleasure or popularity, but it has an important difference—the ultimate concern is beyond self.

It is this motivation that causes Barnabas to answer when asked why he visits a prisoner, "Because I thought I might help him." It is almost a naive answer, full of surprise that the question should be asked.

Barnabas has perceived the Christian truth that it is

in setting aside of self that wholeness of self is gained. This begins with surrender to God. "Surrender to God, not man," he qualifies it. "It doesn't do any good to surrender to man, any man. But you've got to make a complete surrender to God."

Willingness to Be Guided

What does that mean? "It means willingness to be guided by God, to say, 'I've made a mess of things.' For the man in prison, that means accepting the fact that he's been wrong and going on from there, guided by God."

But what does "guided by God" mean?

"It is nothing more than doing what's right," answers Barnabas, who then thinks about that for a time. Then, "I suppose men come to what is right in different ways, but what I mean by an attitude of willingness to be guided by God is the willingness to do what you know is right, not to compromise or go against what you know to be right."

He is not satisfied with his own explanation. He fusses with his pipe and stares out the window. Finally, "I don't know if I know exactly what prayer is, but before I go into a meeting, I pray. I pray to get my attitude right, rather than that I will win my point. Oh, I pray that I can present what I think is right in a way that it will be accepted, but it's more important to get my attitude right. Then if somebody else turns out to be right, I'm in a better position to accept his judgment. I don't have to keep pressing my point so far I jeopardize the whole cause."

Barnabas does not understand such surrender as weakness. "When you put your faith outside yourself, in God, you get the strength to wait."

How did Barnabas put into action his decision to try to do something about the plight of people in institutions?

First, he faithfully served his own prison term until he was released.

Second, he went right back to his old business in stocks and bonds and began to work at building his customers' confidence in him. To this day, forty years later, he openly advises people who entrust their funds in his care that he has had a prison experience. He tells them of his experience as a Christian. He tells them of his record since then. Since his return from prison, Barnabas has sucessfully built two thriving businesses.

Third, he returned to church. He became not just a nominal church member, but a committed and working church member. His own local church has over the years made him one of the official board members, a member of their finance committee, and a representative of their church in ecumenical work in the life of the community as a whole.

Fourth, Barnabas became actively involved in the life of his own political party and began to make his presence known in relation to all the institutions of care and rehabilitation in his state. He did not restrict his attention to prisons only. He spent great quantities of time as a member of a bipartisan board of advisers to the child welfare department of the state government. Many would see this as a "secular" and "political" operation. To the contrary, Barnabas saw it as a way of carrying out his promise to God to "try to do something about" the conditions of life of those in institutions—orphanages, delinquency treatment centers, mental hospitals, prisons.

Fifth, Barnabas set about organizing other laymen into representative panels of Christians who would devote their time, energy, money, and influence to the betterment of conditions in public institutions. One of the most visible ways they accomplished this was to get promises from each successive set of candidates for power to keep the chaplaincy a nonpolitical, merit appointment based upon the specific training of the prospective chaplain and upon the dedication of the person to Christ and his church.

This involved vast amounts of time, energy, and money on Barnabas' part. He traveled all over the state visiting these institutions, conversing with and encouraging chaplains, wardens, superintendents, and commissioners. He knew these people intimately and cared for them deeply. He collaborated with theological schools in his state and fostered the programs that train chaplains for their work. He heartily sustained training programs for theological students in the care of the residents in all kinds of institutions. He never asked anyone for money for his ventures as I have described them. Rather, he used his own funds, drove his own car at his own expense, and paid his own long distance telephone bill out of his own pocket. I estimate that he must have spent at least seventy-five thousand dollars in these efforts.

When Barnabas started his work, there was not a trained, nonpolitically appointed chaplain in any of the institutions in his state. Now there is not an institution that does not have such a chaplain. They are organized into a chaplains' fellowship, and Barnabas is officially elected as "the chaplain of chaplains!"

Finally, Barnabas implemented his commitment by refusing publicity and staying behind the scenes. He committed himself never to take public credit for decisions but to see to it that public officials who made them upon his request got the credit. He also vowed never to give unfavorable public criticism to officials, but always to deal

with problems on a private, face-to-face basis. The commitment to no publicity released the defensivenss of public
officials under the persuasive reasonableness of Barnabas.
He became a trusted friend of governors, commissioners,
superintendents, and wardens.

The sustenance, encouragement, and support Barnabas
received from his wife gave him the inspiration needed to
stay at his task. She traveled with him over the state and
was a known and loved member of the gatherings of chaplains, politicians, inmates, and business people. They were
together, people with a vision empowered by prayer.
Barnabas lost his wife in death a few years ago. The loss
of her was a heavier blow, it seems, than the loss of his
"respectability quotient" through imprisonment. Yet the
vital prayer life engendered during his prison years has
carried him through this greater grief over the loss of his
companion.

Another writer, during the time Barnabas' wife was alive,
describes their comradeship:

At 4 o'clock some afternoon this week, Barnabas will
close the big Standard & Poor's book of business statistics
he has been reading, move the potted plants over by the
window where they can get more light, turn out the lights in
his roomy office, and walk down the hall toward the
elevator.

As he leaves the building, homebound officeworkers will
shout "See you tomorrow" to each other and rush for buses.
He will drive with the rush traffic to his home to pick up
his wife. She will be ready.

They will drive for an hour or two out into the state,
to some prison or mental hospital or children's institution.
There he will meet with a group of men, while she waits
uncomplainingly in the lobby of a hotel. After a long time,

the meeting will break up, and they will drive back. It will be after midnight when they get home.

A group of laymen and ministers gathered in the privacy of a hotel room in the state capital city under the leadership of this man Barnabas. They had an appointment with the governor who was to sign a formal agreement, officially establishing a merit rated chaplaincy for all the institutions operated by the state. No one suggested prayer until the group was ready to go. Then Barnabas, in a shy and unassuming manner, said: "I guess we'd better talk with God before we talk with the Governor." The group prayed together. The prayer and the later signed agreement were the high moments of realization of the commitment Barnabas had made decades before in the yard of the state prison. An unbearable detour had been turned into the highway of the Lord.

When Barnabas is asked if he does not take a great deal of satisfaction when he sees the development of the chaplains program, he always says that he is not the one to receive credit, but rather, he gives credit to prayer that at each step he be given wisdom and guidance in his effort.

CHAPTER IV

Albert Einstein: High School Dropout

Through the use of statistics, our culture has seen to it that a person who drops out of high school is stigmatized. Statistically speaking, he is consigned to the heap of societal failures. He is perceived as retarded, incorrigibly delinquent, lazy, a ne'er-do-well, etc. If he drops out of college, he is perceived as being consigned to doing nonprestigious, menial, poor-paying work. He may be perceived as not being "college material," which may mean that he is too stupid to think abstractly, verbally, and creatively.

Statistically, these stereotypes may be true of large populations of people en masse. However, we have a scarcity of statistics on people who did not conform to the system, did not join the crowd of the public and private educational system, and "struck out on their own." The words *struck out* have a double meaning: first, they can mean failure. A batter up at bat strikes out. Or second, "struck out" may mean to head off in a fresh direction which one quite suddenly sees for himself or herself. Some dropouts from high school or college *really do* fail at many of the tasks of life, of which school is just one. However, some dropouts do just the opposite: they strike out on their own and become trailblazers, pioneers, inventors, discoverers for the rest of the crowd.

Albert Einstein was the latter kind of dropout. He not only dropped out, he was kicked out of the Gymnasium— the European equivalent of our high school. "Einstein was summarily expelled on the grounds that 'your presence in the class is disruptive and affects other students.' " [1] His biographer, Ronald W. Clark, describes the youthful Einstein as "the precocious, half-cocksure, almost insolent Swabian of youth . . . the boy who knew not merely which monkey wrench to throw into the works, but also how best to throw it. This may well explain why the Gymnasium was glad to send him packing." [2]

Einstein, at the age of sixteen, was urged by his father to forget his philosophical dreaming and apply himself to a sensible trade. The youth had no certificate for entering the university, and only trades were open to people without university training. The possible way out of this dilemma was to go to Zurich, Switzerland, to the Swiss Federal Polytechnic School. The principal of the school was impressed with Einstein's mathematical ability and arranged for him to go to a Swiss cantonal school for a year to get ready to pass the entrance exams for the polytechnic school. He finally gained entrance.

However, his experience in what we would call college was filled with a "prickly arrogance" on his part. He became a very awkward scholar, and there was serious question as to whether he would graduate. One of his professors told him that no one could tell him anything. He himself felt stifled by the atmosphere of the school. He says: "The coercion had such a deterring effect [upon me] that, after I had passed the final examination, I found the consideration

[1] Ronald W. Clark, *Einstein: The Life and Times*. Copyright © 1971 by Ronald W. Clark. Used with permission of the publisher, Thomas Y. Crowell Company, Inc.
[2] *Ibid.*, p. 20.

of any scientific problems distasteful to me for an entire year." [3] He did indeed graduate in 1900, but then he encountered another of life's detours: unemployment.

The polytechnic school employed other students and/or helped them to get a place elsewhere. They refused to do either for the difficult fellow, Einstein. Einstein says: "I, a pariah, discounted and little loved . . . was suddenly abandoned by everyone, standing at a loss on the threshold of life." [4]

Einstein became a Swiss citizen, and, like so many young persons of today, was immediately called upon for military service. He failed the physical examination. Therefore, he began seeking a post as a teacher with the result that he got a temporary teaching post, filling in during the military service of another teacher. This post lasted only a few months. However, Einstein was elated. He said: "I am beside myself with joy as I have just received confirmation that all is settled. I have no idea who recommended me, because as far as I know not one of my teachers has a good word to say for me, and I did not apply for the post but was invited." [5]

Yet, the job was very temporary; and then Einstein found himself unemployed again. He made a formal application to the Swiss Patent Office for the post of engineer, Class II. Because of the benevolent dictatorship of the director, who liked Einstein's being a self-confessed "curious bird," he received the job as a Technical Expert (Third Class) on June 16, 1901. He gave thanks for this rather routine and minor position. He said that it gave him freedom of mind in his off hours to pursue his own interests.

---

[3] *Ibid.*, p. 39.
[4] *Ibid.*, p. 40.
[5] *Ibid.*, p. 44.

It kept the wolf away from the door while he did his intellectual work undisturbed. Einstein felt that the practical
job was a salvation for a man of his type. He observed
that the academic career of professor-types "compels a
young man to scientific production, and only strong char-
acters can resist the temptation of a superficial analysis." [6]

Nevertheless, this "marking time" kind of job was a
detour for Einstein. We get the picture of an orthodox city
clerk, going to the Patent Office at a fixed time in the morning and returning to his lodgings in the evening. Yet behind
the scenes he was in his room quietly working toward discovering the laws of nature. While he was a clerk in one
of the "innumerable ruts occupied by minor members of
the Swiss civil service," marrying, and becoming a father in
1903, Einstein was completing the original formulation of
the theory of relativity. He was then, in 1905, twenty-six
years of age. He had only indirect access to scientific
journals which he read in isolation:

Thus from 1902 until 1905 Einstein worked on his own, an
outsider of outsiders, scientifically provincial and having few links
with the main body of contemporary physics. This isolation accounts for his broad view of specific scientific problems—he
ignored the detailed arguments of others because he was unaware
of them. It also shows a courage beyond the call of scientific
duty, submission to the inner compulsion which was to drive him
on throughout life and for which he was willing to sacrifice
everything. [7]

The rest of Einstein's story is better known by far than
are his more obscure vicissitudes with the school systems of
his day. In his later life, Einstein said of schools: "The
worst thing seems to be for a school to work with methods

---

[6] *Ibid.,* p. 51.
[7] *Ibid.,* p. 60.

of fear, force, and artificial authority. Such treatment destroys the healthy feelings, the integrity, and self-confidence of the pupils."

Some Results of the Detours

The kind of experience Einstein had in school could have produced a kind of destructiveness that would have done him and those around him much harm. It could have crushed his spirit, branding him as a failure for the rest of his life. He could have accepted the world's evaluation of him as a failure. The real tragedy would have been that his confidence in his own personhood would have been destroyed. Thus failure could have become an external evaluation of others adopted as a way of life.

Another form this acceptance of failure as a way of life could have taken would have been to "join up" with other so-called failures and to "pool" inferiorities with them. Einstein refused to think or act in "packs" like wolves. He walked alone. How did he handle the "detours" from the angle of vision of the life of the Spirit?

The Stewardship of Loneliness

Einstein said that he was suddenly abandoned. He stood alone. Instead of letting loneliness become depression, Einstein *used* the loneliness for meditation, the idle time for reflection, the mental energy for observation of the world around him. Carl Sandburg said that loneliness is an essential part of a man's life and sometimes he must seek it out: "One of the big jobs a person has is to learn how to live with loneliness. Too many persons allow loneliness to take them over. It is necessary to have within oneself the ability to use loneliness." [8] This using loneliness can be called "the stewardship of loneliness." Einstein's first spiritual discipline was this kind of stewardship.

The Power of an Inquiring Mind

Einstein's frustration with school systems and teachers was not frittered away in petty rebellion. He was not so much a rebel as he was one who had a persistent curiosity that refused to be pushed around. He insisted on turning aside from traditional explanations to listen to the music of the spheres themselves, the nature of motion in relation to motionlessness, and the qualitative character of as well as the quantitative need for energy itself. Rudolph Otto said that the experience of the holy in life is characterized by a sense of mystery and a sense of fascination. As Ronald Clark describes the religion of Einstein, Einstein said that he believed in "Spinoza's God who reveals himself in the harmony of all that exists, not in a God who concerns himself with the fate and actions of men." [9] God was behind energy. Yet, Einstein's actions of mind reflect a patient and persistent search for the meaning of "all that exists" as its internal forces are related to each other. In Martin Buber's words, he answered Buber who pressed him by saying: " 'What we (and by this 'we' he meant we physicists) strive for,' he cried, 'is just to draw His lines after him.' " [10] Ten years later, Einstein said: "I want to know how God created this world. I am not interested in this or that phenomenon, in the spectrum of this or that element. I want to know His thoughts, the rest are details." [11]

---

[8] *Louisville Times*, January 18, 1966, Section B, p. 1.
[9] Clark, *Einstein: The Life and Times*, p. 19.
[10] *Ibid.*, p. 18.
[11] *Ibid.*, p. 19.

A Perspective of Humor

The perception Einstein had of himself included the capacity to laugh at himself and his circumstances in life. He could say wryly that "God is subtle, but he is not malicious." He sent an article he had written to a very especially loved uncle and said the article was his "modest attempt to overcome laziness in writing which I have inherited from both of my dear parents." He spoke of himself as a "curious bird" and as being "not much with people." During all his frustrating reversals in trying to get a job, he could say of himself: "I don't let a single opportunity pass unheeded, nor have I lost my sense of humor. . . . When God created the ass he gave him a thick skin." [12]

Genuine Care

Einstein's winding pilgrimage made both a careful and caring person of him. One era—the last one—was spent in this country at Princeton University. The memory of his own painful experience in school returned to him as an old tape to be replayed when a young girl sent him a manuscript to read. He replied: "Keep your manuscript for your sons and daughters, in order that they may derive consolation from it, and—not give a damn for what their teachers tell them or think of them."

Yet, it was a little elementary-age schoolgirl in Princeton who went home and told her mother that a happy old man had sat on a park bench beside her near the school, and they had fun working her arithmetic problems together. Upon inquiry, the mother found that the old man was Albert Einstein.

---

[12] *Ibid.*, p. 46.

CHAPTER V

A Broken Courtship
As a Life's Detour

Dating and courtship can be for many people a very casual, superficial, and even frivolous experience. For others, it is a search for salvation. For such persons, courtship becomes a life-shaking, life-changing, and life-directing experience. Persons like Dean Inge could carry on their life vocation and sustain a joyous, longsuffering, and adoring relationship to their mates. However, for other persons like Anton Boisen and Soren Kierkegaard, the breaking of a courtship and the frustration of their desire to be married was an anguishing change of direction in their lives. Yet out of their suffering came a totally new kind of definition of purpose, through which they ministered to multitudes of people out of the crucible of their own suffering.

Anton Boisen and Alice Batchelder

Anton Boisen was a Protestant minister. Before he entered the ministry, he was a forester. He met Alice Batchelder at Indiana University where she was the secretary of the Young Women's Christian Association. He says:

She was at that time twenty-two years of age. She was somewhat above average height, with wavy hair of a genuine golden color. What she said [in a speech she was making] I do not remember, but she spoke in a clear, well-modulated voice, and I

50

was impressed with her sincerity and earnestness. I fell in love with her then and there. It was a one-sided affair, a love that swept me off my feet. I received little encouragement, but I saw her from time to time as often as she would let me.[1]

As a forester he spent much of his time thinking of her as he did his work in the woods. While working on the eastern shore of Maryland, he finally, after three months, rallied enough courage to write her. She did not answer him. Later he took a job in her native state with the fond hope that being near her he could see her. He went to see her without announcement of his coming and received a very chilly reception.

This was a religious issue with him. He went to church and heard a sermon which made a clear distinction between following a certain course because of arbitrary desire and doing so in obedience to God's will. He began to search for God's will in the matter. He tells of being prompted on one sleepless night to write Alice, "I rose almost mechanically and wrote to Alice, telling her of the moral struggle I had been having and of my reason for studying forestry." [2] After writing this letter, he read the scripture closely and came to the conclusion: ". . . my love for her was really a desperate cry for salvation and an appeal to a beloved person stronger than myself." [3] In the feverish ideas that surged in his mind, he found one that had special meaning for him. It came to him as follows: "You have found the hills where the flowers grow. It must be your task to show the way to them." [4] He says, "This for me was the call to the

---

[1] Anton T. Boisen, *Out of the Depths* (New York: Harper & Row, Publishers, 1960), p. 52. Used by permission.

[2] *Ibid.,* p. 55.

[3] *Ibid.,* p. 55.

[4] *Ibid.,* p. 56.

ministry." Therefore, he perceived his personal salvation, his love for Alice, and his call to the ministry as one unbroken piece of cloth. They were inseparably woven together.

The consequent story tells of Boisen's repeated attempts to write Alice to get some sort of response from her. On one occasion, she had read his letters with much distress and asked him not to write her any more or to think of her any further. He says, "I felt myself dashed to pieces. It was as if I had been trying to fly and had been brought crashing down. I gave way to a reaction of weakness and despair." [5] When Boisen wrote to Alice telling her of his purpose to enter the ministry, strangely enough she consented to see him again. At this meeting she offered a prayer in his behalf and asked for wisdom and guidance. He wept at the close of her prayer and kissed the hand that she offered him. She said at that time, "God's promises always come true." He took this as a virtual promise of her love. She later said that he had misunderstood and that she had not promised him and that her answer of "no" to him was final and could not be changed.

At this time Boisen's emotional life went into a severe reaction to personal failure. He says: "Then it came to me that even though I had fallen, even though I was a broken vessel, I might give her to someone else." [6] He even turned to one of his fellow foresters and asked him to be that person. He felt that he was very happy and that he had won a great battle. He pulled out of a possible psychotic episode at this time and reorganized his life around his theological education. In the meantime, Alice consented to correspond with him during his seminary years.

---

[5] *Ibid.*, p. 57.
[6] *Ibid.*, p. 59.

Although Boisen "puts himself down" and thinks very lowly of the work he did, he and his steadfast friend, Fred Eastman, did some very vigorous and creative pastoral work in inner-city and rural pastorates. He suffered many reverses, rejections, and yet learned very, very much. My own estimate is that he did a very great deal of good for a lot of people as a theological student who insisted on putting what he was learning into practice.

All this while, however, nothing was changed as far as Alice was concerned. He says:

> I felt myself to be in the situation of a man who has ventured to climb to some great mountain, and finds himself in mid-air, unable to get any foothold or any refuge. To find some validation of the faith which had led me, I was ready to grasp at anything. The very fact that Alice refused me any satisfaction left me, I felt, with no alternative but to strive to become in some measure worthy of her. Never once did I entertain the thought of giving up.[7]

Boisen entered World War I and served with the overseas Young Men's Christian Association among the first to be sent to France. He was assigned to combat units and traveled with the units that saw action at Chateau-Thierry, Saint Mihiel, and the Argonne, and marched with them to the Rhine.

All the while he was in the war zones he had no contact with Alice. Yet all through the war the thought of Alice had been with him. Upon returning home, he went to Chicago to see her but found her adamant in her refusal to see him. He was dazed with the seemingly impossible ending. But he says that he did not give way to the reactional

---

[7] *Ibid.*, p. 72.

weakness as he had earlier. He simply remained in Chicago and pleaded with her.

Boisen took a position with the Inter-Church World Movement in Fargo, North Dakota. When he went there, he began to write to her regularly, a plan to which she gave her consent. She wrote him several times, explained her willingness that they should be friends, but was wanting it clearly understood that it could be nothing more. He replied that he "had rather have just her friendship than the love of any other woman in the world."

Boisen planned to enter the pastorate. He completed his theological education at Union Theological Seminary in New York with an exceptionally good academic standing. Yet he describes the dilemma of the single minister:

> Churches were not too plentiful, especially for a man whose record as a pastor had been no better than mine. Wherever I was being considered, the first question was likely to be, "Are you married?" and the second, "Do you expect to be married?" Neither of these questions could be answered in the affirmative. I would then be told that I must be content with a "modest" church. This meant, I soon discovered, a salary so low as scarcely to permit marriage if things worked as I still hoped they might. It seemed as though I had come up against an impassable wall.[8]

In the face of this kind of large "detour" sign, Boisen collapsed in a total psychotic break with reality. He tells the story in detail of his great suffering in a mental hospital. He says that many persons' only hope for salvation lies in their love for some good woman. In that fact lies hardship and suffering for the woman. Such a demand causes a real loss to society, since it would be only the finer type of woman who would be moved by such an appeal. Boisen's

---

[8] *Ibid.*, p. 77.

psychotic episode meant to him an effort to find a new way out of this dilemma. The psychotic ideation of his illness reflects a curious effort of his to do something that would offset our present system as one of competition and status seeking in sexual mating. His thinking became extremely grandiose. He felt that he represented a personality which for nineteen centuries had been trying without success to solve this dilemma of courtship and marriage. He thought of offering up himself as a sacrificial gift for someone else who could solve the problem, such as his father.

Boisen directly relates his psychotic collapse with the total frustration he experienced in relation to Alice and to his chosen vocation. Yet in the fiery trial of his illness he began to see that though he was "insane," not all of his ideas were completely out of touch with reality. He saw his illness as a struggle between sin and salvation, as a search for redemption. Also he found in his illness a new vocation: that of searching out the relationship between mental illness and authentic religious experience. He says:

> I have chosen deliberately to follow the thing out. I have been following a trail which has taken me through some very dangerous country. But I believe it has been worthwhile, and I would make the same choice again. Even this experience, painful though it is, may be an adventure of which use can be made.[9]

In order to shorten this finely written but somewhat long story, let me say that Boisen never was able to win acceptance by Alice Batchelder. She continued a single life herself. She became ill, was somewhat disabled for a time, and then died. Her death was the occasion of another psychotic episode as well as the publication of his first book in 1937. He dedicated that book, entitled *The Ex-*

---

[9] *Ibid.*, p. 102.

ploration of the Inner World, to her. In the last paragraph
of his autobiography, *Out of the Depths,* Boisen says:

> My mind goes back to the dedication of my *Exploration of the
> Inner World,* which was written during the searchings of heart
> which I underwent at the time of Alice's death. I recognize that
> I was suffering at the time from a deep sense of personal failure
> and that my normal judgment was impaired. Nevertheless, I con-
> sider that dedication to be a true expression of my deepest feeling
> and best insight.[10]

The Dedication of *Exploration of the Inner World* reads
as follows:

> To the memory of A.L.B. For her sake I undertook the adventure
> out of which this book has grown. Her compassion upon a wretch
> in direst need, her wisdom and courage and unswerving fidelity
> have made possible the measure of success which may have been
> achieved. To her I dedicate it in the name of the Love which
> would surmount every barrier, and bridge every chasm, and make
> sure the foundations of the universe.[11]

He considers this dedication to be a genuine expression
of his deepest feeling and best insight. He says: "My love
for her has been linked with all that is best and holiest in
this life of mine." [12]

Boisen was one of my teachers. He never married but
took up a kind of work as a minister that no one else would
dare touch. He became one of the first mental hospital
chaplains. He was convinced that theology should be
studied, not after the experiences which gave it birth had
been written in the books and the books were gathering

---

[10] *Ibid.,* p. 210.
[11] Anton T. Boisen, *Exploration of the Inner World* (New York:
Harper & Row, 1936), from the Dedication. Used by permission.
[12] Boisen, *Out of the Depths,* p. 210.

dust on the library shelf. Theology, the study of the ways of God with men as they seek their way in life's pilgrimage in a wilderness of the lost, should be studied when these experiences are actually happening to people. Persons themselves are the textbooks of theological inquiry. They are "the living human documents."

Boisen, with the collaboration of persons like the superintendent of the hospital where he was a patient, William Lowe Bryan, C. McFie Campbell, Harry Stack Sullivan, and many others pioneered in this field. He later was appointed as a research professor at Chicago Theological Seminary and taught students from there in his work as Chaplain at Elgin State Hospital. It was at this place that I met him.

Contrary to his overly modest estimate of himself, Boisen was a highly disciplined research man, a student of the best opinions in the field of psychiatry and social work, and a writer of massive proportions. He did not see his students as counselees but as collaborators in the search among the wilderness of the lost; namely, mental patients. He insisted that we appreciate the struggle against sin for salvation, the struggle with the temptation to give up and surrender, and the struggle to find the new way of life which was represented in the so-called illness of many of the patients.

Boisen became the founder of what is today known as the Clinical Pastoral Education Movement. That movement created a major revolution in theological education; and if it does not fall back into a methodological sterility, will continue to make a lasting impact on lives of theological students in the future. I give thanks for this new direction that this bachelor-minister took. He was brokenhearted over his loss of his adored loved one. He could not "settle" for anyone else. No one else would do. Therefore, he could not find his way into the "successful" and traditional pastoral ministry. He slammed up against a heavy wall that redirected his life, through severe suffering, to a new way and a new day in the ministry of pastors. He took us as students intensely seriously and never failed to give us appreciation for our contributions in life. I record his story here as a way of honoring my former teacher and giving thanks for this wise old man.

Soren Kierkegaard and Regina Olsen

I turn now to a second person who experienced a life detour in a broken courtship. However, this courtship moves somewhat differently. It is that of Soren Kierkegaard in his relationship to Regina Olsen. He too had committed himself to the ministry as a prospective Lutheran pastor. During his studies, he permitted himself one diversion and that was the thought of a young woman named Regina Olsen. She had been confirmed in the church, was full grown, and he could appropriately think of making his case with her. Concerning his love affair, he said: "Before my father died I had already decided upon her. He died. I read for the examination. During this time I let her existence twine itself about mine." [13] Then again on a later date he wrote:

The period of falling in love is surely the most interesting time, during which (after the total impression has been made by the first stroke of enchantment) from every encounter, from every glance of the eye (however swiftly it takes hiding, so to speak, behind the eyelashes), one fetches something home, like the bird

[13] Walter Lowrie, *A Short Life of Kierkegaard* (Princeton: Princeton University Press, 1942). Copyright 1942 © 1970 by Princeton University Press, p. 131. Used by permission of Princeton University Press.

which in its busy season fetches one piece after another to its nest
and yet constantly feels overwhelmed by the great wealth at its
disposal.[14]

Lowrie says that in addition to the motives which
ordinarily prompt a lover, Kierkegaard "had the hope that
by Regina he would be reconciled with the universal. It
was his only hope for a happy and normal life on earth,
and it was a desperate hope." [15] Kierkegaard expresses this
desperation in his words: "The only thing that comforts
me is that I might lay myself down to die and in the hour
of death confess the love I do not dare to reveal so long as
I live, and which makes me equally happy and un-
happy." [16] He writes concerning his loved one:

Thou, my heart's sovereign, "Regina," treasured in the deepest
privacy of my bosom, at the source of my most vital thought—
where the distance is equally great to heaven and to hell—unknown
godhead! Oh, may I really believe the reports of the poets that
when one sees for the first time the beloved object he believes
that he has seen her long before, that all love, like all knowledge,
is recollection, that in the particular individual love also has its
types, its myths, its Old Testament? Everywhere in the face of
every maiden I see traits of thy beauty, but it seems to me as
though I must have all maidens in order to extract, as it were,
from all their beauty the totality of *thine;* that I must circumnavi-
gate the whole world in order to find the region I lack and which
yet is indicated by the deepest secret of my whole ego—and the
next instant thou art so near to me, so present, replenishing so
mightily my mind, that I am transfigured before myself and feel
that it is good to be here. . . .
    . . . Oh, I will cast everything from me in order to become light
enough to follow thee.[17]

[14] *Ibid.,* p. 131.
[15] *Ibid.,* p. 131.
[16] *Ibid.,* p. 132.
[17] *Ibid.,* p. 132.

Yet this lyrical love went through a torturous transformation into agony, tragedy, and total frustration. The first phase of it culminated in his actually winning her approval and her devotion in which she overwhelmingly wanted to marry him. The success caused him to fall into despair; and during his engagement he fell into a severe debate with himself, became profoundly melancholy, and suffered in his conscience for having "dragged her out with him into the current." He felt divinely vetoed in his desire to marry Regina. Deep underneath this was his feeling that she deserved someone much better than him, that he had brought with him the intolerable melancholy of his father and that although he was a delightful person to be with on a temporary basis, he would be intolerable to live with day after day and over the pull of the years.

Regina vigorously sought to keep him in the engagement and to love him. She demonstrated a womanly and almost worshipful devotion, he says. But he decided that the engagement must be broken and sent the engagement ring back with a brief letter:

In order not to put more often to the test a thing which after all must be done, and which being done will supply the needed strength—let it then be done. Above all, forget him who writes this, forgive a man who, though he may be capable of something, is not capable of making a girl happy.[18]

He felt that if he had let himself get married to her he would have been playing the tyrant, would have been a scoundrel, and that he would have taken advantage of her genuine desire to marry him and in doing so, been a poor steward of her trust in him. He says:

---

[18] *Ibid.*, pp. 138-139.

About me (and this is at once the good and the bad in me) there is something rather ghostly, which accounts for the fact that no one can put up with me who has to see me in everyday intercourse and so comes into real relationship with me. . . . essentially I live in a spirit-world. I was engaged to her for a year, and still she did not really know me. So then she would have gone to smash. . . . I was too heavy for her, and she was too light for me.[19]

The end of the story is that Regina continued to love and admire him although she later married another man.

Soren Kierkegaard, emotionally dying daily over his love for her, lived on for fourteen years, encountering death in his early forties.

However, in these fourteen years Soren Kierkegaard devoted himself to that "spirit-world" of which he spoke. In the extensive writings he produced, he laid out the greatest panoply of poetic wisdom of any theologian and philosopher of our time. He became the originator and vital spirit who stimulated more biblical reflection than most other teachers of the last two hundred years. I personally have profited by his rich contribution, especially in his classical devotional book, entitled *Purity of Heart Is to Will One Thing*.

In both Boisen's and Kierkegaard's instances, one can see the way in which the encounter of men and women with each other in their desire for each other as man and woman can be an infinitely serious kind of thing. One does not find in them the petty triviality of much that is misnamed courtship today. One does not see in them a casual or "flip" attitude about the great issues of human relationships in their depths. Rather, one sees in them the search

---

[19] *Ibid.,* p. 140.

after the face of God, the Creator, who made man and woman for each other and in His own image. These two men were denied the earthly experience of married love. Yet, they became bachelors by choice for the kingdom of heaven's sake. In doing so, they discovered a new direction in life, revealed to married people how casually and pettily we can handle our marriage relationships, and provided us with an understanding of God's love and concern as revealed between the sexes. Hosea's tradition—in a different sense—is continued in these men's relationships to women whom Boisen called "the finer type of woman."

CHAPTER VI

Finding One's Way
With a Handicap

A far larger number of persons than is visibly evident have been deflected from their original directions by physical handicaps. Many people bear incalculable amounts of physical pain. Only those nearest them know about it. Other people, such as colostomy patients, suffer no great amount of pain but have a whole different set of private habits. Diabetics have to rearrange many cultural rituals that involve eating because of their dietary limitations, need for insulin, etc. Asthmatics live altered lives because of breathing handicaps. Recovered cancer patients have to face what one such patient called the "ghoul squad," i.e., those who, upon learning their friends have had cancer, simply assume that such persons are marked for an immediate death.

Such persons as I have mentioned here bear their handicaps covertly. They are more or less isolated by the private rituals of their handicaps. They may be a double responsibility to parents, husband or wife, sons and/or daughters. The larger world reaps the benefit of such persons' labors.

However, there is a considerable part of the population whose public *and* private relationship to their meaningful community, their ability to work, and their own image of themselves are massively rerouted because of physical handicap. These latter persons are our concern here.

I want to tell you how the lives of three persons whom I personally know were blocked and frustrated by an organic handicap. They took a detour into new directions as a result. They witness to God's grace working after the fact of their disabilities by the way they reinterpreted his new directions for their lives.

The spiritual compensation of handicapped persons is a much taken-for-granted fact as we perceive outstanding world figures. A Theodore Roosevelt overcomes the handicaps of early illness and weakness to become a "Rough Rider" in the military. An Eleanor Roosevelt, who perceived herself as an "ugly duckling" in her early years, offset this to become one of the effective political leaders of her day, both in relation to her husband and in her own right both before and after his death. Franklin Delano Roosevelt himself lived a "deflected direction career" after being crippled by poliomyelitis. In addition to his profound impact as President of the United States, he was the moving spirit behind the great medical efforts to conquer polio.

A less well-known person such as Kate Smith, the singer of folk and patriotic songs of World War II, was unusually large and overweight. She is quoted as having decided early to sing so well people would listen to her rather than look at her. Yet, one of the assumptions that tends to accompany many such illustrations is that wealth, fame, and position are the reward of perseverance when faced with an inevitable life detour. One of the main concerns of this discussion of life detours prompted by a physical handicap is to challenge this assumption.

Therefore, let me tell you of three persons whom I know who "won strength from handicaps" and yet have lived modest "nonfamous" lives nevertheless. All three of these persons have very deep relationships to many people, but are not famous or prestigious people who have to worry about their "image" before the mass media, the public eye, or any such thing. They are people who safely appear abroad because they have learned the discipline of solitude, prayer, routine, and being "out of sight." Yet their invisible ministry is greater than many people's service who are always in the public eye.

Virginia Kreyer

The first person I want to introduce to you is a woman whom I have known for twenty years. She was born with the handicap of cerebral palsy. Through the wisdom of caring parents, Virginia learned to use all her intact faculties. Her parents neither let pity for themselves nor an inordinate need to help her cause them to render her helpless in ways she could help herself. She learned to walk—with difficulty. She learned to talk—with difficulty. She learned to relate herself lovingly to her peer group— apparently with joy and ease. She went to school and "kept up" with her class through hard work, always resisting the temptation to "use" her handicap to play on other people's sympathies.

Virginia finished university with high honors and chose to go to theological school because she felt that God had a special destiny for her that called for theological education. She became intensely interested in the pastoral ministry to persons who, like herself, were beset by cerebral palsy. Upon graduation from theological school, she became the chaplain of an institute for the reeducation of cerebral palsy victims. She is an ordained minister in her denomination. She has held this position for about fifteen years as of this writing.

She did not feel that her education in theological school prepared her adequately to meet the complex needs of cerebral palsy patients. Therefore, she continued her education at the New York School of Social Work and received her Master of Science in Social Work.

In writing about the care of cerebral palsy persons, Virginia says:

> The essential attitude which the cerebral palsied person must adopt, if he is to succeed at all, is an acceptance of all that he is and is not. Even though a cerebral palsied individual may have been helped by parents and others in childhood to accept his limitations, when he reaches adolescence and adulthood, feelings of resentment toward his condition and the question, "Why am I handicapped?" is often reopened. Of course, no one would deny that a person who has been taught to accept his limitations in childhood will have less difficulty working through this problem than will a person who has never been helped to accept himself. But in either case, the sympathtic minister can render invaluable assistance.
>
> It has been observed down through the centuries that those who have accepted their handicaps and triumphed over them are those who have learned to look beyond themselves for help. It has also been observed that when an individual does this he not only comes to accept his own suffering or handicap, but learns some of the ways of the spiritual world, and thus comes to see real meaning in his own suffering.

Howard Rees

Another quiet witness to the power of God is a poliomyelitis victim, Howard Rees. This man was studying law at George Washington University. Polio had already done its work, leaving him crippled, in much pain, and walking only with the help of two canes. He was racked with pain, exhausted by its incessant demands, and his hopes shriveled as he drove himself onward. Then two great events took place.

The first event was a happening in prayer. As Howard Rees walked by Calvary Baptist Church in Washington,

D.C., he read a sign inviting him to come into the sanctuary for private meditation and prayer. He went in to pray. During his experience of prayer, Howard Rees discovered that God's power would enable him to surmount his pain with the power of radiance given through prayer. This did not mean that the pain would go away. It meant that he, Rees, would be enabled to transcend it. Yet the lifeline of his power to transcend would be regular, disciplined prayer. Howard Rees committed himself to the new path of prayer which raised him *over* his great obstacle of pain.

The thirty years I have known Howard Rees reveal a man of joy, radiance, and profound influence. He became the director of student religious life, under the auspices of the Baptist denomination, in the colleges and universities of Washington, D.C., and the surrounding area. He has been the sustaining spirit of a steady procession of students who have been introduced to Jesus Christ as Lord. As a professor in a theological seminary, I have met at least twenty or twenty-five theological students who attribute to Howard Rees their indebtedness for their guidance into and growth in the Christian ministry. However, Rees himself is not an ordained minister. Howard Rees is in the tradition of the disciples who never saw themselves "specially ordained" but as responding to the leadership of the Holy Spirit on an hour-by-hour, day-by-day basis. To Howard Rees, the witness to the transforming power of Jesus Christ is a *function* of dedicated persons, not a *social status,* a position, a form of prestige. Yet, it has been miraculous to see how young men and young women have identified with this layman and been encouraged in their commitment to and preparation for the formal Christian ministry.

A second great event took place in Howard Rees's life. He met and married a strong, beautiful, and Christian woman, Sue. She became not just his alter ego; she became an extension of his body. Yet she brought a brilliance and competence of her own to the marriage. All that has been said about Rees's influence is also a comment on Sue's witness through the home. The students whom they influenced met in their home. These intrepid explorers of the Spirit caught the best use of the small group before "groups" were the "in" thing to do.

Both Howard and Sue have been combined influences in the leadership of students. Sue is the "in-the-flesh" answer to Howard Rees's prayer. His commitment to a life of prayer and God's gift of Sue to him have turned the roadblock of polio into a detour that has become a pilgrimage of triumph for him.

Zettie Walters

A third handicapped person whom I want you to meet is a deacon, choir member, and Sunday school teacher. His name is Zettie Walters. He lives in Kannapolis, North Carolina. He worked as a clerk in a department store until his retirement. He sold shirts, ties, and socks, etc., to the men and boys of the town. His powerful witness for Christ had a way of "separating the men from the boys," though.

Zettie Walters is crippled in one leg and walks with a severe limp. I have known him since 1935, but I have never heard him refer to his being crippled, nor have I heard anyone else do so. Yet he has been crippled ever since I have known him. Furthermore, Zettie Walters stammers in his speech. I have seen him teach a Sunday school class, become "tangled" in his speech, and start all over again. Yet the young men whom he taught knew that he knew God personally. We knew that he cared deeply for us in the name of Christ.

Zettie Walters did not just make speeches *about* religion. He stayed in touch with members of his class for years after they "graduated" into new age groups. When they left the area and went elsewhere to school or to other jobs, Zettie kept up with their whereabouts. He sent them messages by others and always asked that they come by to see him when they came back to town. He supplied for each of us a "lasting bond" of loyalty and devotion to God and to the church. He taught us how to mean this same thing to others.

Zettie Walters has been a guide and friend of nearly forty educated and dedicated pastors who "got their start" in the church in which Zettie is a deacon and teacher.

I personally am one of these ministers and pastors. Zettie Walters has followed my life through thick and thin for thirty-seven years. He encouraged me to continue my education. He cosigned the only small loan I made while I was in college. I had to renew the loan often, but I finally got it paid. Yet Zettie was right there all the while.

Not only did Zettie give me financial support. He was a "continuity person" in my home church amid several changes of pastors. Pastors, meaningful as they were, came and went. Zettie's most recent ministry to me was at the death of my ninety-one-year-old mother. He was one of the first to visit us at that time. What I am trying to say is that what Zettie Walters has meant to me, he means to countless other people. His radiance and affirmation of the providence of God extends to others in such a way that no one perceives him as a handicapped person.

Some Common Attributes

All three of these handicapped persons reflect several common characteristics.

First, no one of them held God responsible for the handicap. They did not ask to be exceptions in the universe. They were strengthened with might in the inner person by God in such a powerful way that God was perceived as a friend and not as a void or an enemy. Whitehead has said that we move in three stages in our relation to God—from God the enemy, to God the void, to God the friend. These three people seem not to have experienced God as either an enemy or as a void, but from the start as a friend.

A second characteristic of these three persons was that through their handicaps each has found a vocation. It seems that every person has limitations of one kind or another. The ingenious attack on the frustrations of handicaps and limitations has a way of building the character of a person around a positive reversal of the handicap. The law of compensation is the source of calling and challenge.

Radiance of being is the third characteristic. Radiance is an outward expression of an inner competence in dealing with pain, unchangeable tragedy, and the dead ends of life. A dead end calls for a detour, often a 180-degree detour. This reversal is very akin to the New Testament meaning of conversion, i.e., a turning around, a changing of direction. Conversion for these three people meant far more than a programmed ritual of walking down the aisle at a revival meeting. To them conversion meant a radical wheeling about of their lives in a desperate matter of life and death. They found a meaning and purpose in life to which they committed their whole lives. Their internal clarity of direction enables them to radiate a kind of confidence and joy that is contagious.

Thus these gifts of God—personal responsibility, a clear sense of vocation, and personal radiance—are made available to people like me through such charismatic spirits.

CHAPTER VII

Can an Infant Face
A Life's Detour?

It seems to stretch the point to suggest that very young infants can be presented with a major, life-altering detour by reason of the situations life throws at them very early. Likewise, this can be true of older children. Let me say that I believe that this happens.

Recently, while on vacation at a beach resort, I saw two vivid examples of this in the making. When I have told you of these instances, I will leave it to you to meditate upon whether or not life's detours are set into rapid motion in people's lives at very early ages. The first instance is that of a little boy about two-and-a-half years of age. I call him "The Little Engineer." The second instance is that of a young boy about ten years of age. I call him "Mr. Interpreter."

The Little Engineer

My wife and I observed this little two-and-a-half-year-old boy (whose name is Keith) as he played vigorously but alone in the shallow pond of water on the beach, formed by a rain-water drainage pipe. He never wandered from this pond of water more than a few feet. He never went near the surf. There was no one to go with him into the turbulent waves. He adjusted himself to playing in the small pond instead.

For four consecutive days, he worked hard at playing in the sand and water. He used a bucket and shovel to move sand from one place to another. He tugged manfully at rocks and threw them elsewhere into the water. He built mounds of sand on the edge of the water. He did his work with an intensity, a concentration of attention, and a seriousness I have rarely seen in a child. He "worked at playing" for as much as six hours a day. He did not laugh or squeal with delight. He simply got the job done. His face was a wizened one of an older construction engineer.

The drama of this little boy's life began to unfold as day after day he continued his busy work in the pool of fresh water at the edge of the Atlantic Ocean. We noticed that he apparently did not lie down and rest, stop to take a nap, etc. He did not get a drink or eat anything. His mother, a friend or relative of hers, and a young seventeen or eighteen-year-old girl (probably Keith's sister) were the adults around him.

These three adults kept an eye on him, but did not talk with him or play with him. The two older women talked with each other, slept, and sun-bathed as they did so. The younger woman and a girl friend of hers spent time with the life guards nearby. When Keith was picked up, talked with or cuddled, the younger woman did it.

For the first three days Keith, the little engineer, never cried or asked for attention. On the morning of the fourth day, a crisis came. Seemingly for no external reason, Keith was crying profusely . He seemed sick. His nose was running and had to be wiped often. My wife said that she felt that he was dehydrated from much sun, much activity, and little rest.

As the little engineer became more upset, the two older women became more impatient. They wanted him to hush crying and to continue his play. They sought to continue talking with each other and sunbathing. Keith tried to climb upon the beach chair with one of them, crying frantically as he did so. He was pushed away by his mother, but after much persistence he was allowed to bury his face in her shoulder. Then he ceased crying. In a few minutes, she set him down on his feet. He returned to "working at playing." The last time I saw Keith he was sobbing and asking to be taken into the arms of either one of the older women. His mother said: "If you don't hush crying, I'll leave you here alone." He sobbed: "No! No! No!"

The younger woman was not around at the time. The two older women continued to rebuke him for crying and refused to hold him in their arms. Finally, they began to pour water on him to punish him. He ran from them and ceased to cry. He again took up his shovel, bucket, sticks, and rocks and solemnly began "working at playing" again.

What was the "life's detour"? The mother and her friend seemed to hold to the erroneous idea that loving a child by cuddling him or her "spoils" the child. We never spoil a child by giving comfort and love, especially when the child is tired. By doing things for a child that it can do for itself, we spoil the child. Keith's mirthless "working at play" seemed to *be* his detour. He sought to be a "good" boy, which means he made no demands for attention or affection. He demonstrated remarkable ability to do this. However, the constant activity exhausted him. He received no reward for his massive effort to be a "good" boy. When exhaustion took over, he was punished. What other alternative remained for a little child to get affection and attention? More work and/or illness. It would be easy for this child to become so over-worked that illness would naturally take over. But this little boy would have to be very sick if he was to be noticed. Yet, is the pattern set? Will Keith be a hard worker, always hoping that some reward of affection and grace, warmth and comfort will—unasked —come his way? Will he get affection as a concession when he becomes ill?

A word of understanding needs to be expressed for the two adult women in this little boy's life. The mother was there without a husband and father. Was he himself away working while she and her eighteen-year-old daughter and her two-and-a-half-year-old son went to the beach? Was he a victim of the Vietnam War, dead or missing in action? Was he divorced from her? Was Keith an "after-thought," unplanned for after sixteen years without additional children? I don't know the answers to these questions, but accurate empathy requires that I ask them. I only know two things: the mother did not smile either, and she seemed to have no real joy to share with her little boy in the short time I observed her from a distance. Yet, a person cannot give that which she has not received.

Keith's play became work. Even then it did not get others' affection and approval. Will he "contribute" to a society that withholds from him? Will withholding be more than taxes for him? His life's detour will be to become society's "ever dependable one" who never cries, never asks for affection, and never gets it if he does. The works of his hands will be used by others, but will they respond to his cry for love?

Martin Luther's early religion was built upon the assumption that he must work to earn the love of God. His greatest detour in life that led him to a personal knowledge of Christ came when he discovered that the love of God was his through faith and faith alone. Then the beauty of the Lord rested upon the works of his hands. Work became an expression of gratitude for the love of God, not a feverish effort to merit the love of God.

I pray for Keith, "the little engineer," that he will discover a love which he does not have to work to earn. I pray that he will be loved for his own sake alone, because of who he is and not because of what he does. Such a discovery will be to him a new direction in life. As it is, his calling to love and to be loved is being detoured into a compulsion to drive himself and be driven to "work at play." When play becomes work, even for a little child, a tragic detour takes place. I pray, furthermore, that he will find an answer for his loneliness in someone who will adventure with him out of the little puddles of life into the exciting breakers of the larger ocean of life and love.

Mr. Interpreter

The second child I want to tell you about is a ten- or eleven-year-old boy. I was checking out of a hotel one morning and this young boy was just ahead of me in the line. He told the desk clerk that his father had asked him to ask her if it would be possible for him and his family to remain in the room in which they had stayed the night before. Or, he asked, would it be necessary for them to take a new room. The clerk said it would be necessary for them to move. The room they were in had been rented to someone else. Then he asked her if the new room would be the same price as the one now occupied. She said it would be the same price.

I wondered deeply why a boy his age would be negotiating for a new room. Why would the father rely on him for this? Most boys that age would be sleeping, swimming out in the hotel pool, or picking at and aggravating one or more of their brothers and sisters.

As I was wondering, the father himself appeared on the scene. He nudged his son and looked at him queryingly, searching his face as if to ask: "What did she say?"

The son then began to talk to his father in sign language, vigorously gesticulating as he relayed the story to his father. He went back through the whole transaction with the clerk, as the son told his father what the clerk said. Then they departed together.

I was caused to meditate on the way in which the course of this young boy's life was being redirected—not by his own handicap—but by his father's deafness. Yet he seems to do this because he wants to and not because he has to do so. Many children would have resisted or not have bothered about learning the sign language. Others would have let the burden rest entirely on their father to communicate by writing notes. Others would have let their mother or another sibling do that while they "did their own thing."

Yet, this boy was different. He chose the direction of becoming a Mr. Interpreter. At a tender age, he began a skill that will diversify and enrich his own life immeasurably. He will be a close observer and listener. He will be an accurate and faithful reporter of what other people say. He will be sensitive to what they *mean* as well as to what they say. More than this, he will understand the mind of his father; and his father will understand his mind in a way other fathers and sons do not. They will have expanses of comradeship denied others.

As I meditated upon the brief scene I saw, I began to sense a parable of our relationship to God. *His* voice is not *heard,* either, the psalmist tells us. We perceive his message through observation, sign, fellowship, intuition, and emotional sensitivity. We convey that message to others as faithful sons or daughters of God. We discover our own calling and new direction in life as we blend "doing our own thing" into communicating his intention to others and into having close fellowship with him.

It seems to me that "Mr. Interpreter" has been detoured away from narcissism into altruism, away from speaking just for himself into speaking for others. I hope that his father is genuinely aware of the "gem of purest ray serene" he has in his son. I hope that generous quantities of admiration and tender affection go from the father to the son. I pray that as the son has disciplined himself to participate in the father's adult world, the father in turn will encourage young Mr. Interpreter to have friends his own age and will as a father get acquainted with these other young persons and their parents. Other parents and children need to know a whole lot of what I learned a little bit of in those seven or eight minutes as I was checking out of a hotel and met but never talked with young "Mr. Interpreter."

CHAPTER VIII

The Detour as a Way of Life

One of the central contributions of the Judeo-Christian faith in God is the persistent expectation that we shall have no other gods before him. We cannot serve two masters, says Jesus. From the vantage point of sustained resistance to the temptation of idolatry, most of the ways in life's pilgrimage which *we* choose *are* bound to demand a detour if we discover the larger purposes of the one God. What is at first seen by us as a dead end, a noisome and bothersome detour, is in fact a diversion of our path away from our own petty idolatries to the great highway of the worship and love of God. Let me illustrate and describe what I mean.

The Broken Marriage

Boisen and Kierkegaard both dimly saw, but did not put into words, that the institution of marriage itself can be a form of idolatry. When a marriage is broken, then many of us act as if there is no hope for the persons before God. Divorced persons, therefore, are subtly ostracized from the life of the church. They themselves are too prone to see themselves as second-class citizens. In many respects, they are treated by society as "outsiders."

Yet, a divorce may just be the end of an idolatry of a particular relationship to a particular person and possibly the idolatry of marriage itself. I have seen persons slam into the grief of losing their marital partner and take a good long while to recover. Then I have seen them discover a new comradeship with God. Their lives have been lived over the pull of the years with a steadfast devotion to God. Prayer comes into their lives to turn their loneliness into solitude, and their solitude into fellowship in ministering to other people. I have seen unorganized but powerfully alive groups of divorcees come into being to form a fellowship of concern for other hurting and brokenhearted persons.

The great griefs of life are often *not* the loss of someone by death. Death itself is definitive, unmistakably final, and easy to see as grief. Such a loss as divorce is haggle-hearted and undefined, remarkably indecisive, and hard to see as grief. Yet, some divorced persons I know have seen their temptations for what they were—to let their broken marriage become a stuttering, sputtering broken record that could play only one note. Therefore, they went on to a larger design and purpose in life and made God the center of their existence. Remarkably enough, they discovered that God loves and forgives and cares for divorced persons in some strangely wonderful and unexpected ways.

Broken Job Relationships

Many people are idolaters of the institution and/or job where they work. Ministers, doctors, and lawyers are notorious worshipers of their professions. When anything goes wrong in their work, idolaters of the job tend to go to pieces. I have seen men and women in their early careers suffer with a massive job failure. I have seen them fold up as human beings and spend the rest of their lives weeping, wailing, and berating others for injustices and indignities heaped upon them. I have seen some of these persons die an early death. They never found that they were idolaters of their jobs; therefore, they never found the larger directions of God for them.

On the other hand, I have seen both men and women stand back from the pieces of their life's work, gain a whole new perspective, and reorganize their lives around a new purpose for which God had called them. They have become some of the more innovative, unique creators of new forms of work. As in the case of divorced persons, these persons cannot easily be identified or described. Their biographies are much too numerous and too personal to describe here.

However, at the time of this writing—August, 1973— the newspapers are full of stories of the tragedies of the careers of men like John Mitchell, John Dean, Jeb Magruder, Patrick Gray, and others in the Watergate affair. Quite apart from partisan politics, human lives of men at work—who have families at home—are at a massive, public detour sign. Indictments, pleas of guilty, possibilities of conviction and/or disbarment from law practice are the order of the day. One cannot but be touched with concern for the personal tragedies involved. Patrick Gray put it most poignantly during his appearance at the Senate hearing when he said in Spanish to Senator Joseph M. Montoya: *"Yo tengo mucho dolor en mi corazon ahora."* Senator Montoya translated: "I have a lot of hurt in my heart at this time." As my morning paper said: "Promising young careers have been cut short. Hard-won older reputations have been soiled. Some face the threat of prison; others, disbarment. Jobs are hard to come by. Attorneys' fees are high. Six men are in jail, one freed on bond. The wife of one is dead."

These men have let their pursuit of success on their jobs become the central passion of life to the exclusion of all else. The pursuit of the jobs has turned into a pursuit of loneliness. Their jobs have collapsed like a "bridge out" on the wrong road. The recovery of a sense of direction, the discovery of a larger loyalty, the revelation of a new purpose in life are good things for which I pray for them. I know both the temptations and the sin of the idolatry of a particular position and a particular institution. Mine are just smaller than theirs. Yet all jobs and institutions are too small to be God in a person's life. The worship of these jobs and institutions almost always leads to a much deserved and needed detour.

I say, "almost always." I mean this. Sometimes people do not learn from experience. They simply redouble their effort and fanatically speed ahead in the same direction. Someone has defined a fanatic as a person who has lost his sense of direction and tried to solve his problem by doubling his speed. They are not like the East Kentucky man who lived to be a hundred years old. When asked his secret, he said, "I learned very early to know when to give up." He said that many people keep flailing away at battles that never should be won anyhow, trying to succeed at tasks that are pointless when accomplished.

This can apply well to many of the noisy word battles that keep people awake nights figuring out what they are going to say the next day and rebuking themselves for not having said just the right, clever, and hurting thing the day before. These fights, be they in business, politics, or at church, are an experiment in idolatrous futility. Amid one such temptation in my own work, I wrote these words several years ago:

> And, they said to me: "Let's fight!"
> And I said to them:
> "What are we fighting about

And what are we fighting for?"
They said: "We are fighting about
This, that and the other."
I said to them: "But what are we
Fighting for?"
They did not answer but
Only snickered and punched
Each other's ribs.

Then I went out doors to
A high hill that overlooked a river
On which gathered ships of the nations.
Then the Lord said to me:
"Do you want to know what
They are fighting for?"
I said: "Yes."
The Lord said:
"They are fighting for
A bucket of ashes, a
Piece of sackcloth
And a cup of gall."
I said: "But what are
These for?"
And the Lord said:
"The ashes are their
Shattered hopes.
The sackcloth is for those
Who repent the futility of the
Fight and find their way to me.
The gall is for those to
Drink who refuse to repent
And never change their way."

Yet repentance is more than just saying "I am sorry." It is giving up—giving up false gods; knowing from the eternal and true God when and how to give up. Then a new direction is revealed because God has one for us and we are now pointed in the right direction that enables us to see it.

Fearing Poverty and Seeking Status

The fear of poverty is another form of idolatry that often underlies the worship of one's job and institution. Persons who came to adulthood during the Great Depression of the 1930's are particularly prone to build their lives around the temporal idol of economic security. The search for economic security becomes entangled with the need for status and prestige. Having the symbols of affluence—land, houses, club memberships, cars, gadgets, etc.—becomes the affluent man's and woman's alternative to the fear of poverty. These symbols of security become increasingly heavy weights upon the status seeker. Soon he and/or she find themselves as persons who have given their hearts away, "late and soon, getting and spending." They have wasted their natural powers. They become practical idolaters of not just economic security out of the fear of poverty, but also idolaters of their own need for prestige, position, and dominance.

Such feverish commitment to things is easily translated into a secular kind of religion. Religious leaders turn great masses of people into willing slaves to church building programs that are far beyond the means of people to finance. They take it so far in some instances that the people are embroiled in legal troubles over the mishandling of money. Elaborate quantities of tithes and offerings can be spent in this sort of "service to the Lord." As Shakespeare in *Troilus and Cressida* says:

> 'Tis mad idolatry
> To make the service greater than the god;
>
> . . . .
>   . . . thus to persist
> In doing wrong extenuates not wrong,
> But makes it much more heavy.

These heavy idolatries are ways of life that collapse of their own weight. Then a new direction for living is required. A person suddenly asks himself or herself: "What is life all about? Why am I a slave to charge accounts, monthly payments, and ceaseless repair bills?" The answer to the question is that such total preoccupation with the symbols of affluence is a "dead-end" kind of existence. It *is* idolatry. The worship of one true God is heard as Jesus Christ calls us from each idol that would keep us.

The call of Christ takes us on a great detour from the idols that keep us. Each such idol must fall of its own weight. Life is simplified and the fear of poverty and love of affluence are replaced by simplicity of desire, life style, and the use of time, energy, and money. We come to the highway of the Lord's making and know that a man's life consists not in the abundance of things we possess or the visibility of the positions we hold. A man's life consists of glorifying and enjoying God.

CHAPTER IX

The Cross of Christ
As a Life's Detour

A book on new directions for the living of these days must be climaxed with a witness to the Lord Jesus Christ's own experiences with detours in his life, death, and resurrection. Judged by the wisdom of the people of his day, Jesus' life on earth ended as a total failure—dying on a cross as any common criminal would die. His disciples were overwhelmed with the seeming collapse of their fond ambition to follow him into "instant greatness." There he was: dead on a cross. His life and their hopes were at an end.

Yet on the first day of the week, something happened. Up from the grave he arose! He had challenged the power of death and through faith in God had found a new way—life through death. He demonstrated the power of God to free us of the idolatry of our fear of death. This idolatry makes us worshipers of youth and health, and despisers of the dying, the aged, and the sick. Consequently, we worship these gods with a backward look into the rear view mirror of our lives as we travel. Hope is turned into nostalgia for the past, and joy in living is turned into cynicism and disgust.

Yet, the life of our Lord Jesus Christ shows that dying to our old way of life and being raised to walk in the newness of life is *the* great detour of human existence. Old things pass away and all things are made new. Paul said that Jesus was in the very form of God, but he took upon himself the form of humanity, dying the death of the cross. Wherefore, God exalted him.

Jesus refused the powers offered him by Satan. He gave up his hopes for an earthly family, the controlling desire of the devout Jewish man even today. Every major move he made was built on the serene assurance that if the low-vaulted temples men build are destroyed, through the power of resurrection they will be rebuilt in a new way according to the design of God. In another figure of speech, he says that if a grain of wheat falls into the ground and dies, it will take root and bring forth much fruit.

Many readers of this book contemplate the meaning of death in its earlier forms. We do not—except in catastrophic ways such as an accident or a combat death, etc.—die all at once. Rather, we die a piece at a time. The appendix goes, the gallbladder is removed, the hearing and eyesight become impaired, the effects of arthritis hinder our ability to walk, and arteriosclerosis hampers our ability to think and behave accurately. Each one of these is a small portion of death, deflecting the directions of life. "Spareparts" surgery has changed some of this, creating at times false or short-lived hope.

In all instances, the Resurrection of Jesus Christ affords us the alternatives to futility in the deification of physical health. The recent literature on "death and dying" tells us that people go through several phases of adjustment to the reality that they are dying: anger, apathy, bargaining with God, despair, acceptance, and hope. In more than a symbolic way, we die a lot in each of the great detours of life. Jesus tells us that if we are to save our lives we must lose them. In losing our lives we discover a new highway of hope in the Resurrection of Jesus Christ.

ABOUT THE AUTHOR

Wayne E. Oates, born in Greenville, South Carolina, in 1917, is Professor of Psychology of Religion, Southern Baptist Theological Seminary, Louisville, Kentucky. Dr. Oates holds degrees from Wake Forrest College and Southern Baptist Seminary. He did postgraduate study at Union Theological Seminary, New York, and University of Louisville Medical School.

With his training, insights, and love of people, Dr. Oates has been an inspiration and a help to many. He has served several rural and urban churches in North Carolina and Kentucky and has been chaplain of both general and mental hospitals in Kentucky.

Dr. Oates has contributed to numerous periodicals and is the author of many books, including *On Becoming Children of God, New Dimensions of Pastoral Care, Confessions of a Workaholic, When Religion Gets Sick,* and *The Psychology of Religion.*

He is married to Pauline Rhodes of Spring Hope, North Carolina; and they have two sons, William Wayne and Charles Edwin.